DISCARD

QC

Extreme Habitats

Desert
Survival

By Jim Pipe

Consultant: Greg Aplet Ph.D., The Wilderness Society

Gareth Stevens
Publishing

Please visit our web site at: www.garethstevens.com
For a free color catalog describing our list
of high-quality books, call 1-800-542-2595 (USA) or 1-800-387-3178 (Canada).

Library of Congress Cataloging-in-Publication Data

Pipe, Jim.
    Desert survival / Jim Pipe. — North American ed.
      p. cm. — (Extreme habitats)
    Includes index.
    ISBN: 978-0-8368-8245-2 (lib. bdg.)
    1. Deserts—Juvenile literature. 2. Desert ecology—Juvenile
literature. 3. Habitat (Ecology)—Juvenile literature. I. Title.
    QH88.P56   2008
    577.54—dc22   2007007943

This North American edition first published in 2008 by
Gareth Stevens Publishing
A Weekly Reader® Company
1 Reader's Digest Road
Pleasantville, NY 10570-7000 USA

This U.S. edition copyright © 2008 by Gareth Stevens, Inc.
Original edition copyright © 2007 by ticktock Entertainment Ltd.
First published in Great Britain in 2007 by ticktock Media Ltd.,
Unit 2, Orchard Business Centre, North Farm Road,
Tunbridge Wells, Kent, TN2 3XF, United Kingdom

ticktock project editor: Rebecca Clunes
ticktock project designer: Sara Greasley

Gareth Stevens managing editor: Valerie J. Weber
Gareth Stevens editor: Tea Benduhn
Gareth Stevens art direction: Tammy West
Gareth Stevens graphic designer: Dave Kowalski
Gareth Stevens production: Jessica Yanke

Picture credits: (t=top, b=bottom, c=center, l=left, r=right)
Suzy Bennett/Alamy 26c; Tim Hurst/Alamy 20t; Robert Harding Picture Library Ltd/Alamy 27b; Peter Lillie/Gallo Images/Corbis 14–15t; Hubert
Stadler/Corbis 11b; Hugh Sitton/zefa/Corbis 27t; Robert Cameron/Getty 29t; NASA 10t; Charles M. Omnanney/Rex Features 13b; Shutterstock
4–5 (all), 6–7, 8b, 10–11, 10b, 11t, 12l, 12b, 13t, 13r, 14–15, 16–17 (all), 18–19 (all), 20b, 21 (all), 22t, 22b, 23cb, 25t, 25cb, 25b, 26b, 27ct, 27cb,
28 (all), 29c; Ticktock Media Archive 1, 6t, 8t, 9(all), 14l, 15r, 23t, 23ct, 23b, 24, 25ct, 26t, 29b. All artwork Ticktock Media Archive.

Every effort has been made to trace the copyright holders for the photos used in this book. The publisher apologizes, in advance, for any
unintentional omissions and would be pleased to insert the appropriate acknowledgements in any subsequent edition of this publication.

Printed in the United States of America

1 2 3 4 5 6 7 8 9 11 10 09 08 07

Contents

Words that appear in the glossary are printed in **boldface** type the first time they occur in the text.

Dry, Hot, and Empty?

The red-barred dragon is a lizard that lives in some Australian deserts.

The ground under your feet is sandy and dry. There are no clouds in the sky, and the Sun is burning hot. Not a sound can be heard and nothing moves. The desert all around you is lifeless . . . or is it?

Look closer, and you will find small mammals and lizards hiding in the shade of a rock. Under the ground, millions of plant seeds wait for rain to fall, so they can sprout.

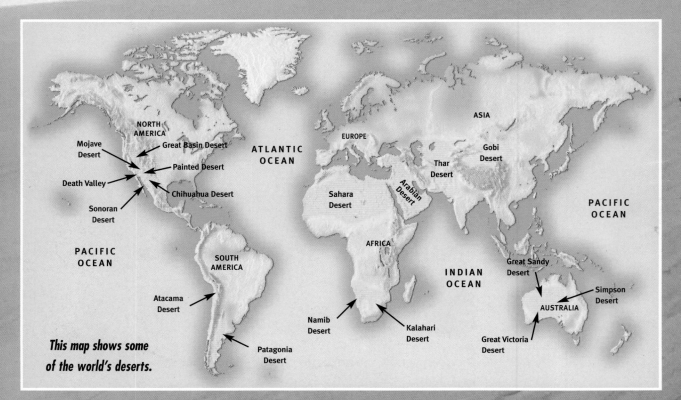

This map shows some of the world's deserts.

In fact, lots of people and thousands of kinds of animals live in deserts. Despite the heat, the lack of water, and blinding **sandstorms**, they survive. Could you?

A desert is a place where very little rain falls. Many deserts are scorching hot. Some deserts can get very cold, however, such as the **Gobi Desert** in Asia. Even during the day, temperatures can drop to −22 °Fahrenheit (−30 °Celsius).

DESERT SURVIVAL TIPS

Even if you do not feel thirsty, drink up! In a hot desert, an adult needs to drink 3 to 4 gallons (10 to 15 liters) of water every day.

Desert Notebook

- By definition, a desert gets less than 10 inches (25 centimeters) of rain or snow each year.

- Only about 20 percent of Earth's deserts are sandy. The rest of them are covered with rocks, gravel, dust, or minerals, such as salt.

Fennec fox

- Even if a desert is extremely hot during the day, it gets very cold at night.

- Many animals such as fennec foxes, kangaroo rats, jack rabbits, and scorpions come out at night.

Journey into the Desert

White clothing reflects the sunlight and helps keep a person cool.

Deserts are beautiful but deadly. In a hot desert, a healthy person left without water and shade for an entire day could be dead by evening.

Out in the open, the hot Sun quickly burns your skin. The heat makes you sweat, so your body loses lots of water even when you are sitting in the shade.

If you are planning a trip into the desert, make sure you bring the right gear! The desert Sun is very harsh and will quickly burn bare skin. Sunblock, light clothes, and wide-brimmed hats will keep the Sun off your body. At night, it can get very cold, so you will also need a thick jacket and sleeping bag.

Travel is difficult. Cars and trucks can sink down in the soft sand.

DESERT SURVIVAL TIPS

Getting lost in the desert is a fatal mistake. You are very unlikely to bump into anyone else! Use maps and a compass to find your way.

Bring water — lots of it! Many expedition groups carry big water containers on trucks. If you do manage to find water, use a **water filter** to make it safe to drink.

Be prepared for extreme weather, such as sandstorms. Lightning can also strike frequently in deserts, even if no rain falls.

Desert Notebook

• Very few desert animals can kill a person, but spiders, scorpions, and snakes can give you a nasty bite or sting.

The poisonous horned adder lives in the Kalahari Desert.

• More people drown in the **Sahara Desert** than die from thirst. Heavy rain can turn dry valleys into surging rivers in a few minutes.

Lightning strikes are so hot they can turn sand into glass. The melted sand forms a tube called a fulgurite.

The Largest Desert

The Sahara is by far the biggest hot desert in the world. It is about the same size as the United States. It stretches 3,100 miles (5,000 kilometers) across northern Africa, from the Atlantic Ocean to the Red Sea. If you get lost in a desert this big, no one will hear you scream!

If you walked across the Sahara Desert, you would find many different landscapes. You would cross **sand dunes**, gravel plains, and rocky uplands. In the middle of the desert, you could even climb tall mountains with snowy peaks!

The huge sand dunes of the Sahara are known as ergs. Sand dunes form where something, such as a plant, blocks the wind, and sand piles up next to it.

Camels carry passengers and cargo in the Sahara Desert.

Ergs in the Sahara often form crescent shapes.

Many desert peoples survive by wandering from one **oasis** to the next. An oasis is a green spot in a desert where plants can grow all year. The Sahara has ninety large oases where people live in villages and grow crops. You cannot always rely on an oasis for water, however. Sometimes the wells run dry.

A river or underground spring usually provides water for an oasis.

Desert Notebook

- Eight thousand years ago, much of the Sahara was covered in grasslands and forests. Cave paintings from this time show giraffes, elephants, and crocodiles.

Cave paintings in the Sahara

- The Sahara is bigger than the next eight biggest deserts put together.

- The world's tallest sand dunes are in the northeastern part of the Sahara. They are 1,525 feet (465 meters) tall — higher than the Sears Tower, the tallest building in the United States.

DESERT SURVIVAL TIPS

Some Saharan scorpions can kill a human with one poisonous sting. In the desert, watch out where you put your hands and feet!

The Ultimate Dust Bowl

The **NASA** robot Zoë collects data from the Atacama Desert.

The driest desert in the world, the **Atacama Desert** stretches along the coast of Chile between the Pacific Ocean and the Andes Mountains. In its very driest areas, scientists have found no signs of life. Not even **bacteria** can survive here. Space scientists visit the Atacama Desert to figure out how they could look for life on the dry landscape of Mars.

Deserts are dry because the ground loses water faster than rain can keep the ground moist. Water drains away or dries up and goes into the air as **water vapor**.

The Atacama is a **rain shadow desert**. A rain shadow desert forms when tall mountains block rain clouds from reaching land on the other side of the mountains. The Andes Mountains block winds blowing in from the east. Clouds release their rain before they can reach the desert.

DESERT SURVIVAL TIPS

Stay out of the hot sun or you could get heatstroke. To prevent vomiting, confusion, and blackouts, drink lots of water and seek shelter. Even the shade of your car can help.

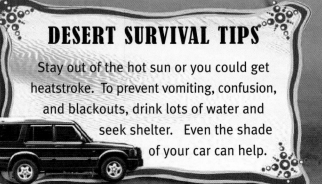

Much of the Atacama Desert is sandy and rocky.

Only a few tough plants can survive in the Atacama Desert. They collect moisture from sea fog that rolls in from the Pacific Ocean. In many years, fog provides the only moisture the desert gets.

Desert Notebook

- Flocks of flamingos live near the Atacama salt lakes. They feed on red **algae** that grow in the water. The flamingos' diet turns their feathers pink.

A flock of flamingos

- In some parts of the Atacama Desert, no rainfall has ever been recorded.

This concrete statue, built in 1992, is 36 feet (11 m) tall. It stands in the heart of the Atacama Desert, and many tourists go to see it every year.

Hot As an Oven?

The equator

Many of the world's deserts are near the equator. Here, the Sun's rays are strongest, and few clouds pass through the sky. Without clouds to shield the ground, deserts are roasting hot during the day and freezing cold at night.

Many deserts are near the equator, which is an imaginary line around the center of Earth.

Many deserts are not hot all year round. Their temperatures change with the seasons. The Mojave Desert in California, for example, may offer hikers a gentle stroll in January and a fight for their survival in July.

Some of the hottest temperatures ever recorded were in **Death Valley** in the Mojave Desert. In 1913, the highest recorded temperature reached almost 134 °F (57 °C).

The smooth, flat surface of Black Rock Desert in Nevada is perfect for seeing which car can go fastest on land. In 1997, a car called the Thrust SSC made the world record for land speed at 763 miles (1,228 km) per hour.

DESERT SURVIVAL TIPS

Is that a pool of water in the distance? Do not count on it! You may just be looking at dry land. Tricks of the light, **mirages** are caused by sunlight on hot ground.

Lakes that have dried up leave behind a large area of flat land.

*The flat, empty desert allowed Thrust SSC to become the first car to break the **sound barrier**.*

Desert Notebook

- The highest air temperature ever recorded was in Libya at Al'Aziziyah. In September 1922, the thermometer measured a blistering 136 °F (58 °C).

- The world's longest heat wave was at Marble Bar in Australia, where the temperature reached 100 °F (38 °C) or higher for more than 160 days in a row.

Some deserts are so hot that you could fry an egg on the rocks.

- The change from blazing heat during the day to freezing cold at night is enough to make rocks crack. Some split at night with a loud bang.

13

Desert Storms

Not all sand is tan, black, or white. A microscope reveals the different colors of sand.

Do you think deserts are calm and peaceful? Think again. Deserts are among the windiest places on Earth. The blazing Sun bakes the ground and heats the air above it. The hot air rises, and cooler air rushes in to take its place. The constant movement of air creates wind — lots of it.

Sandstorms can leave a thick coating of dust and sand on plants, animals, and houses.

Fierce desert winds create amazing rock sculptures. The sand wears away soft rock first, leaving hard rock standing.

The speed and direction of wind changes constantly. The changing wind creates arches and giant stacks of rock, as well as strange-looking pillars and mushroom shapes called **hoodoos**.

DESERT SURVIVAL TIPS

If you get caught in a sandstorm, place a wet cloth over your nose and mouth to help you breathe. Grains of sand will blast at your legs, so wear long pants.

These rock formations are in Monument Valley in Arizona.

Desert Notebook

- In some parts of the Gobi Desert, strong winds blow all year, pushing the sand along. Even the biggest sand dunes move about 164 feet (50 m) each year.

Two kite buggies race across the desert.

- In 2006, one sandstorm in the Gobi Desert carried 330,600 tons (300,000 tonnes) of sand. The storm dumped the sand on Beijing, China, which is more than 1,000 miles (1,600 km) away!

The Coldest Deserts

ANTARCTICA

• Dry Valleys

*If you crossed the deadliest desert in the world, you would not have to worry about heat! Just 4 inches (10 cm) of snow falls on **Antarctica** each year, making it a desert. Antarctica is so dry that some parts are completely free from ice.*

As well as being the coldest desert on Earth, Antarctica is also the windiest, highest, most isolated, and least explored continent. If you want to explore an extreme habitat, look no further! In winter, temperatures in Antarctica can fall to −126 °F (−88 °C), making it the coldest place on Earth.

Some places in Antarctica have not had any rain for four million years! The **Dry Valleys** of Antarctica get almost no snowfall or moisture — they are drier than the Sahara Desert. Thousands of years ago, the mountains blocked **glaciers** from moving

The Dry Valleys in
Antarctica cover about
1,850 square miles
(4,800 square kilometers).

into the valleys, leaving large areas of bare rock. Today, winds swoop through the valleys, quickly blowing away any moisture.

The Gobi Desert is another cold desert. In winter, temperatures average −40 °F (−40 °C). In northwestern China, a region of the Gobi Desert is called the Takla Makan Desert. Its name means "Go in and you will not come out again!"

Wild camels in the cold Gobi Desert survive by eating snow rather than drinking water.

DESERT SURVIVAL TIPS

If you need to move cargo across the Gobi Desert, bring a camel! The camels of the Gobi Desert can walk 30 miles (50 km) a day while carrying 310 pounds (140 kilograms) of cargo.

Desert Notebook

- The mountains of the Gobi Desert are home to the beautiful snow leopard, which hunts wild sheep, mountain goats, and rabbits. Few people have ever seen this shy animal in the wild.

Snow leopard

- There are cold deserts in many parts of the world. The Great Basin Desert in the western United States is a cold desert.

- In the Atacama Desert in Chile, daily temperatures often drop to freezing!

17

Desert Wonders

The Vermillion Cliffs in Utah are named for the red-colored minerals in the rock.

Even if you survive the heat, dust, and wind of the desert, you might not get over its beauty! You can climb tall pillars of rock, explore deep canyons, and walk across sand dunes shaped like crescents or stars.

The largest single rock in the world is in the central desert of Australia. Known as Ayers Rock, or Uluru, it is about 1.2 miles (2 km) long and 1.5 miles (2.5 km) wide. At different times of the day, the rock appears to change color from blue to violet to glowing red! It is considered holy by the local Anangu people, and ancient paintings decorate its cave walls.

If you visit the Painted Desert in Arizona at sunrise or sunset, the rocks and sand will shine in a rainbow of colors. The colors range from purple to yellow and from brown to red.

Deserts are full of surprises. In the Atacama Desert, you will find the amazing El Tatio **geysers** at an elevation of 14,100 feet (4,300 m). These geysers shoot pillars of water and steam 16 feet (5 m) into the air. In the nearby hills, the Chiu-Chiu Lagoon is 490 feet (150 m) deep. It is a lake right in the middle of the desert!

Ayers Rock, or Uluru, in Australia looks like it glows at sunrise and sunset. It is made of a type of sandstone that makes it look red hot.

El Tatio geysers spew steam in the Atacama Desert in Chile.

DESERT SURVIVAL TIPS

Avoid walking across a desert during the hottest hours of the day. Plane-crash survivors have walked more than 340 miles (550 km) in twenty days by walking only at night.

FACT FILE:

Plant Survivors

Only the toughest plants can live in a desert. Most are built to collect and store water. As a result, desert plants look different than plants living in other habitats.

Desert locust

- Plants that store water often grow sharp spines to stop desert animals from eating them.

- After a rainstorm, seeds sprout, grow, and bloom in just a few weeks. They can turn even the driest desert into a carpet of colorful flowers.

- When rain falls in some dry areas of Africa and Asia, it can trigger a giant swarm of desert locusts.

- A swarm contains billions of locusts, and they eat everything in their path, including food crops for people. Local people can have a food shortage after a locust swarm.

HOW DO CACTI SURVIVE IN THE DESERT?

Instead of leaves, cacti have sharp spines that stop animals from eating them.

Folds along the cacti allow them to swell up with water when rain falls.

Their tough, waxy skin seals in moisture.

Cacti grow slowly, and some can live for two hundred years.

*Cacti can survive years of **drought** on water collected from a single rainfall.*

Tough Plants

- **Welwitschia plants**
  - This plant has leaves that grow up to 13 feet (4 m) long. The leaves collect water from nighttime sea fog and send the moisture to the plant's roots.
  - It lives in the Namib Desert in Africa.
  - Some plants may live for two thousand years.

Welwitschia plant

- **Baobab trees**
  - This tree has no leaves for most of the year. The leaves sprout only during the short rainy season.
  - Its large trunk stores water for the nine dry months of the year.
  - It is native to Africa and Australia.

Baobab tree

- **Jumping chollas**
  - This cactus has stems that fall off so easily that they seem to jump out and bite you when you pass.
  - The roots of a 3-foot (1-m) tall cholla cover an area the size of a tennis court.

Jumping cholla

The desert paintbrush survives in the dry desert by taking water from the roots of neighboring plants.

Animal Survivors

Desert animals need special bodies to cope with the dryness, the baking heat during the day, and the bitter cold at night.

The red kangaroo from Australia can go for months without drinking at all.

- Smaller animals survive by avoiding heat. The tiny elf owl shelters from the hot desert sunlight inside a saguaro cactus.

- Larger animals survive by moving around and will travel a long way from one **water hole** to the next.

- Many desert animals have pale skin, feathers, or fur. Light colors reflect the Sun's heat better than dark colors, keeping them cool.

How are people and camels adapted to survive in the desert?

	PERSON	CAMEL
DAYS IT CAN LIVE WITHOUT WATER	1 day	20 days
AMOUNT IT CAN DRINK IN 10 MINUTES	2 quarts (2 liters)	26 gallons (100 liters)
EYELASHES (TO PREVENT SAND IN EYES)	1 set	3 sets
ABILITY TO WALK ON SAND	Bad – feet sink in sand	Good – has tough soles and spreads its weight on four broad feet
OTHER ADAPTATIONS	The ability to use tools and fire and to work in groups means that people can live comfortably in the desert.	Camels have a hump that stores fat for times when food is scarce. They also have a pale coat to reflect the Sun's heat and a tough mouth to eat spiny desert plants.

Tricks for Survival

- **Jerboas**
  - The jerboa's long legs help it move quickly over the hot desert sand.
  - It gets its water from seeds, so it does not need to drink.
  - It does not sweat, and it has very dry droppings.

- **Honeypot ants**
  - Honeypot ants gather nectar from flowers during the rainy season and feed it to special worker ants.
  - These workers store the nectar in their bodies. During the dry summer season, they spit out the nectar for the rest of the colony to feed on.

- **Sandgrouses**
  - A male sandgrouse will fly as far as 100 miles (160 km) every day to find water.
  - It soaks up the water with its belly feathers. Then it flies home, bringing the water to its thirsty chicks.

Jerboa

Honeypot ant

Sandgrouse

- Pale colors are also a good form of camouflage, helping an animal blend in with sand or rocks.

- Some animals avoid the hot Sun by going underground. The spadefoot toad spends most of the year in a deep burrow underground. It only comes out during the rainy season to lay its eggs.

Spadefoot toad

FACT FILE:

Desert Hunters

The gila monster is the largest North American lizard.

Even big hunters, such as lions, can survive in a desert. They get water from the blood of their prey. Many predators living in a desert hunt at night and keep cool in rocky dens or burrows during the day.

- Some desert animals, such as king snakes and geckos, have large eyes that are perfect for hunting at night.

- Other animals, such as scorpions, use their senses of touch and smell to hunt in the dark.

DESERT FOOD WEB

This diagram is a simple food web. It shows how desert predators rely on other animals for food. The red arrows point from the food or prey to the animal that eats it.

hawk

fennec fox

lizard

mouse

spider

beetle

seeds

Desert Predators

- ## Vultures

  - Vultures escape the midday heat by soaring high into the cool air.
  - While flying, they look for sick or dead animals to eat. They can smell a dead animal from far away.
  - They sometimes cool their legs by peeing on them!

Vulture

- ## Sidewinder snakes

  - This poisonous snake moves over hot sand in a special way so only a small part of its body touches the hot sand at any time.
  - It hunts by burying itself in sand and waiting for prey.
  - After a sidewinder bites a warm-blooded animal, it will let go of the animal and hunt it down later.

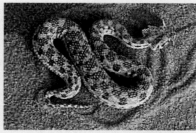

Sidewinder

- ## Roadrunners

  - A roadrunner can fly, but it usually walks or runs.
  - This bird can run 17 miles (27 km) per hour.
  - It runs fast enough to catch a rattlesnake. The roadrunner snaps up the snake by the tail and slams its head against the ground until it is dead.

Roadrunner

- Many desert creatures, such as snakes, scorpions, and spiders, have poisonous bites or stings. Food is difficult to find in a desert, and poison stops their victims from running away!

A rattlesnake may rattle its tail to warn possible predators that it is poisonous.

FACT FILE:

Desert People

Surviving in the desert depends on finding food and water. In the past, desert people stayed alive by moving from place to place. They camped wherever they stopped.

The Mongols of the Gobi Desert use a type of tent called a yurt for shelter. They can easily move the yurt, which is helpful for a nomadic people.

- Some desert people, such as the Bedouins and the Tuareg, are **herders** and **traders**.

- Camels, goats, and sheep provide **nomadic** people with meat, milk, wool, and skins.

- The San people of the Kalahari Desert live in family groups and hunt small mammals.

- Native Australians hunt and gather their food. They look for food, such as wallabies, **witchetty grubs**, insects, and berries.

Sometimes, people eat witchetty grubs raw!

Wallabies live throughout Australia.

These peoples live in the world's major deserts.	
PEOPLE	**DESERT**
BEDOUINS	ARABIAN
NATIVE AUSTRALIANS	AUSTRALIA
MONGOLS	GOBI
SAN	KALAHARI
TUAREG	SAHARA

Bedouin Survival Techniques

- **Headcloths**
  - A headcloth is wrapped around the head.
  - It shields out the Sun and provides protection against the cold.
  - One end can be brought up to cover the nose and mouth to keep out the wind and sand.

- **Tracking**
  - Tracking is a traditional skill, and the Bedouin people used it to hunt wild animals.
  - A Bedouin person may be able to identify the footprint of a relative as easily as you would recognize a friend's photograph.

- **Collecting water**
  - Just before the Sun rises, Bedouins will turn over stones that are half-buried in the desert sand. They collect the fine drops of water that form on the stones' cool undersides.

A Bedouin man wearing a headcloth

Footprint

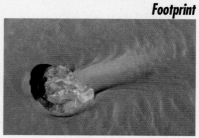

Stone in the desert

A Native Australian woman digs for grubs, which are a good source of protein.

FACT FILE:

Desert Threat

Deserts are unsuitable land for farming because they do not have enough water to grow crops. Poor farming techniques are making land near deserts unsuitable, too. These techniques increase areas of dry land and weak soil in a process known as **desertification.**

- The areas near deserts are at risk of desertification. People must be careful when farming the land.

- People often cut down trees along the edges of deserts. Without trees, the desert land spreads.

Windmills like this can pump water in desert areas.

Why are deserts spreading?

People herd animals on the edges of the desert.

Animals eat plants and the soil becomes thin and dry.

Without plant roots to hold soil in place, it blows away.

Soon, nothing can grow at all. The desert has spread.

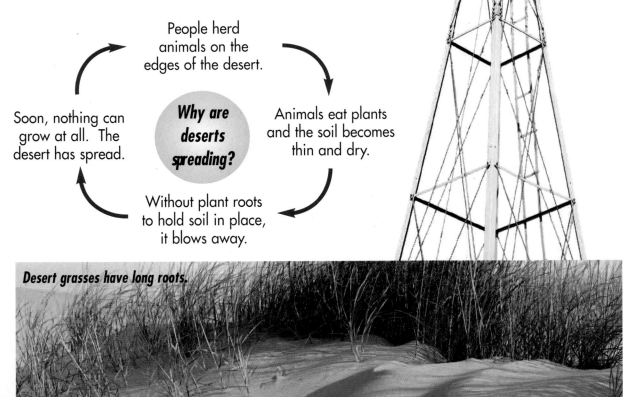

Desert grasses have long roots.

28

Desert Problems

- **Groundwater**
  - Many people live in cities in desert areas, such as Las Vegas, Nevada.
  - Modern cities need lots of water.
  - Machines pump water from deep underground up to the desert surface.
  - Water may be used up faster than it can be replaced by rain or other sources.

- **Roads**
  - Big animals, such as mountain lions, need large, wild areas to roam, away from cars and humans.
  - Cities and busy roads make it difficult for big wild animals to survive.

- **Mining**
  - There are many riches in the desert, such as oil, minerals, gold, and diamonds.
  - Mining creates a lot of pollution.
  - It also causes **soil erosion**, leading to desertification.

Las Vegas

Mountain lion

Mining

This map shows the areas around the Sahara Desert that are at risk of becoming deserts.

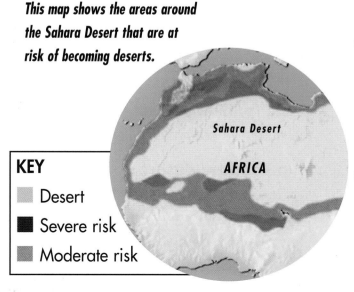

Sahara Desert

AFRICA

KEY

- Desert
- Severe risk
- Moderate risk

- Some people are working to slow the spread of deserts. They are planting trees and tough grasses on the edges of deserts to hold the soil in place.

- In some areas, **canals** transfer water from lakes and rivers to desert areas.

29

Glossary

algae – simple plants that live in water

Antarctica – the continent surrounding the South Pole. It is the world's largest desert.

Atacama Desert – a dry desert in Chile in South America. It is long and narrow, about 95 miles (150 km) wide and 620 miles (1,000 km) long.

bacteria – single-celled life forms that live in soil, water, and the bodies of plants and animals

canals – waterways that are built to carry boats or to take water from one place to another

Death Valley – a desert in California and Nevada that receives less than 2 inches (5 cm) of rain per year

desertification – the process of fertile land shrinking as land becomes desert

drought – a long period during which very little rain falls

Dry Valleys – an area in Antarctica that is not covered with ice and snow

equator – the imaginary line around the middle of Earth. It divides the globe into a southern half and a northern half.

geysers – hot springs that shoot water and steam into the air

glaciers – large masses of ice

Gobi Desert – a large desert covering parts of China and Mongolia in Asia

herders – groups of people who keep herds of sheep, goats, horses, and/or camels. They are often nomads and follow their herds to new grazing pastures.

hoodoos – unusually shaped rocks that are formed by the wind wearing away the soft parts of the main rock

mirages – images of objects, such as oases, that are not really there. Mirages are caused by heat bending light rays from the Sun.

NASA – short for National Aeronautics and Space Administration, the U.S. organization that sends astronauts into space

nomadic – describing a group of people who do not settle in towns and villages but instead move around in search of food for themselves and their herds of animals

oasis (plural: oases) – a place in the desert where water is found

rain shadow desert – a dry area that forms on one side of some mountains. If winds usually blow from one direction, the mountains block rain clouds and very little rain reaches the other side.

Sahara Desert – the largest hot desert in the world. It lies in northern Africa.

sand dunes – large hills of sand

sandstorms – strong winds that pick up tons of sand and blow it around

soil erosion – the result of soil being washed away by rain or blown away by wind

sound barrier – a speed faster than the speed of sound

traders – groups of people who make their living by buying and selling goods

water hole – a pool of water in a dry area

water filter – a device that catches dirt, while tiny holes allow clean water to trickle through

water vapor – tiny droplets of water in the air

witchetty grubs – large wood-feeding moth larvae found in Australia

For Further Information

Books

Desert. Earth's Biomes (series). Tom Warhol (Benchmark Books)

Desert Habitats. Exploring Habitats (series). Paul Bennett (Gareth Stevens)

Trapped in the Desert!: Aron Ralston's Story of Survival. True Tales of Survival (series). Matt Doeden (Capstone Press)

Web sites

Missouri Botanical Garden.
mbgnet.net/sets/desert/index.htm
Click on the links to find out more about desert life.

Desert Kid Outdoors.
www.kidcrosswords.com/kidoutdoors/where%20to%20go/desert.htm
Click on the links to find out about desert animals, famous places, and more.

Publisher's note to educators and parents: Our editors have carefully reviewed these Web sites to ensure that they are suitable for children. Many Web sites change frequently, however, and we cannot guarantee that a site's future contents will continue to meet our high standards of quality and educational value. Be advised that children should be closely supervised whenever they access the Internet.

Index